Fists of Rage

Fists of Rage

Arketa Williams;
Ti'Ara "TI" Walpool

Copyright © 2015 by Arketa Williams; Ti'Ara "TI" Walpool.

All rights reserved. No part of this book may be reproduced or transmitted in any form or by any means, electronic or mechanical, including photocopying, recording, or by any information storage and retrieval system, without permission in writing from the copyright owner.

Contents

Acknowledgements vii

A Scripture for You...1
Bondage 4
Closed Capture 5
Kareen 7
Child Custody...9
I Am a Statistic...11
Corrupted Neighborhood..12
You Are Me 13
Abusive Love 14
Lies 16
Everyday Problems 17
Just A Struggle 18
Suicide 19
Ten Count...20
Breaking Through Secrets Never Told.................................22
He Cried 26
You Don't Say 27
If You Wasn't My Cousin 29
Tug-a-War 31
Normal 33
The Stories Lie Within The Pages 35
Stained..37
There Was A Way Out 38
You Gon Get This Work 40
Beaten Woman's Syndrome 41
The Mirror Was Always Hidden 43
Porcelain Doll 44
Take a Deeper Look 45

Nigga Get Gone 46
I Didn't Need Marks To Remind Me How Much I Hated Myself...48
Tornado 51
Pain, Suffering, and Sorrow...53
Troubles Don't Last Always 54
Let Me Be Me 55
Brain Surgeon 57

Resources 59

Acknowledgements

As always, I want to thank God for bringing me off of such a difficult journey. For gifting me with the ability to creatively discuss the road travelled in a unique way that can inspire, motivate, and encourage others. Thank you to those of you who gave me a reason to write. Those of you who attempted to shatter, destroy, and break me but called it love. Had it not been for you, I never would've known the magnitude of my strength or the depth of my weakness. Thank you Sunshine for being the bright light that shined in some of my darkest places. For showing me what it truly meant to love myself, for lending a shoulder to cry on during my difficult moments, and for guiding me through the mending phase of my broken pieces. To those of you who prayed for me, stood in my line of fire as I tried to escape, and held me close to you when discouragement and defeat set in to devour me. Thank you for not letting me go. To those of you who pulled me out of the darkness and guided me to the power of my voice… THANK YOU!

Arketa Williams

First and foremost, nothing can be said or done without thanking God. I used to curse Him and be so mad, but I thank Him for the many tests and for bringing me out. I pray that He helps me touch at least one person. To my family and friends who have been there for me even when I wasn't there for myself. The prayers and late night conversations of reassurance and telling me everything will be ok- I love ya'll. To my brother John, thank you for introducing me to the concept of poetry. Jocelyn thank you for forcing me to share my writing and listening to thousands of poorly written words. Quayce thank you for holding my hand, dream chasing with me, and never letting me run away. We have come a long way. The both of you are blessings and sisters I always needed. To Dexter - rest in peace. I love you and wish you were here to see your "track star" show her poetic side. Thank you for always encouraging me! I have to thank the people who gave me the stories and words that needed to be written. Thank you to the amazing man who really did not mean to break me. I forgive you. The guy I had to see on campus after cutting my insides, it still hurts sometimes, but I no longer fear the tears. As well as the people I will always forgive because I know no other way to live. I understand what you did not at the time. If it weren't for you I would have nothing to say. Thank you to my aunts who gave me the courage to speak up. Mommy and Daddy, I love ya'll with everything in me. Our time was cut short but I promise I will still make ya'll proud. Thank you for being my guardian angels and fueling me with the power to write.

Ti'Ara "TI" Walpool

This is for every secret hidden by fear, shame, and defeat too scared to step into the light and be told. I pray that as you walk our path with us throughout these pages it encourages you to find the strength you need to get help. You are not alone in your darkness and you don't have to fight this battle alone. We have seen many dark places, stood head to head with the real life monsters, and survived. You can too. Step into your freedom.

A Scripture for You

I know you didn't mean to kill her
I imagine that your finger just slipped on the trigger
That you were so full of hatred and revenge
malice and venom
That somehow you let a fucking $20 debt cloud
your mind & twist your judgement
To take the life of a mother of two
But I know you really didn't mean to
I know you were only hoping to scare her
So she'd go running back to daddy and tell
him that they was looking for him
That you were after him
Because everybody knew you were the local neighborhood drug dealer
And I'm sad to say that I knew my father
somehow played a part in this
Even though he didn't mean to he was involved in this

But I know you didn't mean to actually pull the trigger
So many times to shoot my mother in her back
To leave her laying in the back parking lot of a Minyards
I know you didn't understand or fathom
the damage that would be done
You were going to give daddy nightmares every night
Because he somehow let you take the only woman he ever loved.
You were going to make my brother feel guilty
Cause he thought it was his fault that momma got shot
And my grandmother would never be able to look at me
because I'd always stare back with eyes just like her
Her. The woman I looked just like but never knew
You see I was only three and you left me without a memory
But with scares of being just like my mother
and like you I never understood

Staring into memories confused and hurt,
I couldn't look into my own eyes
But if I could look at you today
I'd stare you dead in your eyes
And ask you..... Are you saved!?
Do you believe in God?
Because I pray that after you killed my mother that you got saved
That you realized that God was real
And you were only serving Him with a purpose and His plan
I hope you gave your soul to Him
Searched long and hard for Him
And I've spent so many years with questions for you
And too many with a hate too deep for you
And God came to me and said I needed to forgive
So that I can finally live and love again
But I hope I see you in heaven
I guess so I could say thank you
The oddest words I'd ever want to say to the man
who killed my mother and broke my family
But I see that there was a purpose and a plan for your hate and venom
And that anger you had over a fucking $20
You see I wouldn't be the woman that I am today
I never would have gotten my life together with God
And I hate that it took losing my mother to your spiteful ass
But I'm gonna continue to pray that while you sit in that cell
That you think about the shit that you've done and
that you get your life together with God
In fact I should write you a letter and send you a scripture everyday
So I know for sure that I'll see you at the pearly gates
Cause I know
With all of my heart I know
Somehow
That you didn't mean to kill her
That your finger just accidentally slipped on the trigger
That you didn't mean to shot my mother in her back
To leave her laying in the back parking lot of Minyards
That you didn't realize you were taking my mother away

So I'm going to pray that somebody takes this venom out of you
That somebody takes this venom and this hate out of you
That somebody takes the hate out of me
Because I know you didn't mean to kill her

Bondage

She never imagined this life to be her life
This place to be her home
Darkness to be her background, the only vision she could call her own
The streets to be her shadows, the crack to give her grace
This drink to be her mercy, abandonment to reflect her face
The broken lines to be her heart, these shattered vocals to be her voice
This pain to be forced upon, but the reaction to be her choice
Life to mirror the silhouettes of the only figure she knew
In order to get close to mama you had to do what she'd do
And though the love was only temporary the connection was very real
Dead man on board walking selling her soul for less than a meal
Grasping hold of the false pretenses of an
artificial peace never to be gained
Weary from self-destruction too lost for dreams to sustain
Looking for acceptance in fictitious idols too afraid to let go for God
Trapped in the bondage of generational
curses turning tricks for tacky jobs
Death making emergency announcements
Satan conducting altar calls for her soul
Wisdom never walking into its future
because misery swallowed it whole
Confined by limitations of white inhaled despairs
Leaving visible trails of footprints in the shadows
of heavy burdens her cross so freely bares
Dear God please find her freedom the peace she and her
Soul never shared. . .

Closed Capture

Come on and come close by with closed
Eyes so you can envision my life
A mile in my shoes and you at my side to show
you why I've lived life dead on the inside
Why I've spent a life time running backwards
trying to leave the past behind
Creating lyrical images with the tears that carved valleys in my mind
With the dream of one day spitting that right rhyme just one time
That would strike a movement in someone's heart
In hopes that it saves the soul like mine that's
been drowning from the start
Let me show you why at three
I was bounced on his knee
while his hands explored my body
Why at six life tripped him, he stumbled between my legs,
and landed in the gap of my innocence
And for years all I knew was survival of the fittest
See for me there was no knight in shining
armor to rescue me from this
My life was predestined for death from the
beginning when everybody spoke it
So come on and close by with closed eyes
to walk down my pathway of life
Let me show you why by nine I knew all the pimps and player's lines
By ten I had been offered up as a sacrifice to him to shine
Where mama failed to meet his needs
Bone of her bone, flesh of her flesh, I was her heir, her seed
And when it came time to make a decision
she chose the crack over me
Ran from her responsibilities to keep from
facing the discomfort of what
stared back at her in the morning
Life's lies that embedded wounds in her heart that strangled her soul

And in the midst of her pain I came
tumbling in to despairs black hole
Born into the injustices of memories that wouldn't allow her to be free
Breath and push, breath and push, she pushed but I wasn't breathing
It was too early and she wasn't ready so I
faded into a disconnected memory
Tangled so that my future and I would never meet
So I grew into a dysfunctional teen living reality as a dream
To keep from feeling the torment of my own memories
So come on and come close by with closed eyes to see the triumphs
I lived through in my life
Let me show you that as an adult I could look
back and see victory in the pains I felt
Although all I saw was the sorrows of being alone
It was then God carried me through the storms to make it grown
And if my stories reach the deaf ears of that inner child in need
I've accomplished the purpose I seek
I've been a light in sometimes otherwise dark places
Using my mess as a message of hope
See I didn't make it this far to hang strangled
at the end of defeats rope
If it was really my time to go I would've died when experiments
And I wrote the book on how to do so
No one ever said that life would be easy nor that it owes me anything,
But I've learned to take from it what I can
So my pictures create lyrical freedoms to show
souls like mine against all odds
You can still stand
So come on and close by with closed eyes so you can envision my life
A mile in my shoes guiding you by my side
walking through hidden memories to gain
Freedom on the inside.

Kareen

I noticed you without actually looking at you
your laugh always rang high and it was piercing
anywhere in the classroom was your spotlight
you were beautiful
I'm sorry that I never noticed you
I overlooked slashes everyday as you hugged me
I missed the ups and downs in your emotions
the days were you plastered smiles to avoid tears
or when you pretended to be sleep
Kareen wake up
Kareen stand up
I need you to work
I regret being consumed by 26 other students
trying to walk a room and address everyone's
questions while ignoring you
the day I saw what razors did to your beauty I wanted to cry
you laughed and played as if you were wonder woman
wondering if anyone else had noticed
there was a promise that you were past those moments
you said the high was no longer needed
I wanted to believe you
it was April 22nd, sixth period you asked me for a Band-Aid
and my soul screamed
I am so sorry I didn't notice
if no one else ever tells you,
I want you to know you are beautiful
intelligence is inside you
I have seen you defeat what you thought was unbeatable
I am proud of you

so every time you pull your sleeves back
don't see what hate did
look at what love can do
remember that those scars can heal
and they're marks to remember why God wanted you to live.

Child Custody

We took turns sharing her
Trying to give each other the same fair opportunity
And that was when I realized I'm too selfish
That I don't want to share
Because sharing is not caring!
It's tearing pieces of myself apart, handing them to you
With nothing in return: no thank you, no hugs
Only me pretending to smile about it
So I called for quitsies and a solution to be made
And we took turns trying to share Love
As if she was some small child caught in a nasty custody case
Problem was she wasn't our child to begin with
And neither of us really wanted her…
Only wanted to pull her away from the other
So the sharing idea was unsuccessful.
We divided up time like we had been two divorced parents
Saying you could have her every other day
Or how about Monday through Wednesday she's yours
And Thursday through Saturday she's mine
Sundays are up for grabs
And I won every Sunday too
I snatched her up so fast
I wanted Love from you
I never wanted to keep her from you
I just simply desired and wished you'd hand her to me
Like the baby girl we pretended her to be, into my arms
So I could cherish her and rock her to sleep
But all we did was argue and fight
Trying to soak up each other's love without giving our own in return
So we battled it out in court
Draining each other's portions of Love
We ruined her life being stubborn and unwilling to realize our
wrongs

That the only reason we had held on
Was because we were both too proud to admit that we couldn't handle love
But instead pretended and played tug-a-war with each other's hearts
Trying to be more determined than the other to draw the love out of each other
But the reality was that the love was never in
Only sitting on the outside since we were deaf and never heard it knocking to come in
So we fought a war for something neither of us had
And we tried to share Love like it was a child
But we ended up tearing her apart with our confusion and wretched mind games
I hope next time we understand
That not every mature decision needs to be made in court
And that real love is not a game
To play with each other's minds, hearts, and souls…

I Am a Statistic

I am a statistic.
I have been a statistic
I will be one again
The same as you

I am the victim of self hate and misunderstanding
I can't seem to take in the concept of who I think I am supposed to be
So I crash into mirrors with hate and pain
And allow blood thoughts to paint my face
like makeup to cover blemishes
My abuse is my blemish

I was a part of the 10 stadiums full of children who were abused
Not the my mother beat me to keep me out of jail type abuse
But actual mental, physical, and emotional abuse
Like how do you take me in as your child?
But never treat me like I am your child
I was deprived from being told I love you everyday by
someone who should have shown and said it in every way
I love you

And those are the reasons I hate myself
Because I never learned that I was to love myself
So my abuse goes further than what people have done to me
I've done more damage to myself than anyone else
I have bullied myself into believing I wasn't shit
Because I was conditioned to based off the way I was treated

I am a statistic
I have been a statistic
I will be one again
The same as you

Corrupted Neighborhood

Cars are passing
Everybody's laughing
At the couple across the street
I shed tears of sorrow
As he beats her in the street
She's his wife and supposed to be treated like a queen
But he beats her senseless as if she never meant a thing
And for the safety of her children
There's nothing she can do
If she leaves he'll kill her
And probably the children too
You can't have him arrested
Because then he'll come after you
So the children grow up in an abusive lifestyle
And all you can do is watch and pray it only lasts a while

You Are Me

Girl looking back in the mirror
I wondered who you were
What you'd been through
Who and what you'd seen
Girl whose voice echoes in my room
I thought about you every time I sung
Tried to understand the pain in your song
But the joy in the notes
Girl who wrote her life within my heart
I promise I'll only whisper your secrets
That I won't use them against you
Cherish and watch over your writings
I'll be your paper
Girl in the mirror
Yea, you looking back at me
Every time you smile I smile
And I hope you continue to
Cause I now know that you are me....

Abusive Love

Here we go again…
There's a cut on my lip
And a knot on my back
And my baby boy is just sitting there mad
While his little sister is holding her teddy bear
With too many tears to share
Do I tell her what my mother told me?
That a man will hit you if you make him mad
So then she grows up expecting to get a back hand slap
Or hiding herself afraid with the wrong man
And how do I explain to him not be like him?
That the number of bruises is not a tally for the amount of love
Love?
It can't be love that's got you hitting on me
While your kids watch crying "no Daddy"
And you only throw them to the side
Screaming "ya momma needs some tough love"
Got me bleeding real red love
So here we go again
The vicious cycle that claimed my mother
And before her, her mother
And I promised myself I'd do better
But somehow your gentle kiss
And sweet words turned into this
Strangling and fist pumping
That doesn't make you more of man
Nor does it teach your son what a man does
So I can only hope and pray that the cycle stops here
'Cause today was the last time
Too many years of hiding my tears
And calling police that don't do nothing
You know, the police will come twice as fast
if I told them that I didn't know you

They said "domestic violence should be a
private thing kept in the house"
But how private are the scars that mark my face
That my sunglasses can't cover
And my lies of being clumsy can't mask
There ain't enough make up to conceal the damage of three lives
Because our daughter might think its ok
for a man to throw her around
Bet you'd be mad then
And our son might just grow up in your steps
Or grow against your walk
Hit me again
I can't hit like a man but he sure can
So here we go again…
Except this time I ain't there to be your punching bag
And the audience ain't your kids
I'm done being a statistic
That one fourth of ladies that are abused before death
And I refuse to be a member of the 2 million battered women's club
Every time you blink a women is abused by someone she loves
Haha love love
Love won't make you hit me the way you do
And love won't make me stay
I'm done with abusive love

Lies

Truth hurts sometimes
But does closing your eyes
Help disguise these lies
Or just blind these cries
While we laid in bed trying to realize
That we're only hurting the people in our lives
With these weak, I'm scared, cover up type lies
These you deserve better than what I'm doing type cries
I love you and can't bare to see you in pain type lies.
Truth hurts sometimes
But doesn't peeling off your fake disguise?
Or is it worth these lies?
Because now a days nobody even tries
And we wonder why hope seemingly dies
There's love and hate in these lies

Everyday Problems

You talk about how I am, but you haven't lived my life
You criticize my ways, but you weren't 20 men's
wife held down and shared from behind
Raped first when I was nine
What a price to pay at sixteen
When my own mama pressed charges against me
All she could say was don't drop the soap that's what I get
But he was raping me and beating her…
death was the only way he'd quit
I was already weak and didn't deserve it
So you talk about switch, but let's talk about
the circumstances that perceived it
Women aren't the only ones robbed of their innocence
Much of what you see on TV I lived it
And just to add a twist the important prominent Pastor did it
Put a gun to my temple and said he'd kill me if I snitched
I prayed to God but where was he in the midst
I tried to get help but no one would listen
His reputation equaled his position
I have rooted on the inside of me a homosexual spirit
And after so many years I just got used to it
But ten years later I still face the same
circumstances I did in the beginning
A midst my heart aches there is no winning
From behind these bars my getting used to's
ascended into cravings I'm baring
My manhood took a road I never saw it sharing
These were my everyday problems
You dislike who I am but when I reached out
no one was willing to help solve them
You pass judgment on me now but this could've been you
So before you ridicule who I am find out what I went through

Just A Struggle

Too tired to move forward
Can't step back
Lost with no direction
All is gone just like that

No control
Yet raging pains
Feelings of loneliness
Mixed with shame

Flipping emotions and nowhere to turn
Yearning for guidance
There's so much to learn

Misery and suffering
Are all a part of life
Which is a daily mission
Mixed with strife

Trying to survive
In this world today
Struggling to live
As we make our way

Through the troublesome times
That we must face
As we travel life's journey
As if it were a race

A race through the hands of time
Trying to stay safe
Without losing your mind

Suicide

I close my eyes
My dreams come true
The world is different
The things are new

I feel the drips
I hear the screams
My body's weak
So what does it mean

My wish came true
I no longer belong
With the rest of you
My life is gone……

Ten Count

One, Two, Three, Four, Five, Six, Seven, Eight, Nine, Ten
BREATHE
Again
One, Two, Three, Four, Five, Six, Seven, Eight, Nine, Ten
STOP!!!!!!
He was doing it again and I could no longer hide under the bed
and pretend that I couldn't hear it because I would see it later
The black eyes
The busted lips
The blue and black finger prints
Left as trophies for me to nurture back to its original existence
I'm done hiding this
I can no longer act like this didn't affect me when it was me
I never meant for this to be
This is not how I pictured me living
Every day running, hiding, only for him to find me
And for everything to repeat again
One, Two, Three, Four, Five, Six, Seven, Eight, Nine, Ten
BREATHE
Again

I have to get out
But how do I escape when he said he loves me
One, Two, Three….
More punches, kicks, me flying now bleeding
His love is going to kill me
One, Two, Three, now breathe
I've got to get free
But he won't let me leave
Six, Seven, Eight, Nine, Ten…
Every time I head for the door he's doing it again
I be damned if I let his love kill me
"Just let me leave don't make me choose"

"You CAN'T whoop me and you ain't getting through"

One, Two, Three, Four, Five, Six, Seven, Eight, Nine, Ten
BREATHE
Again
STOP!!!!
I'm not sure when I ended up here but it's come down to my life or his
Pissed
Ain't no ring on it so if death is the way you
want to go I'm willing to help you get it
The same trophies he left on me I found the strength in the objects
I was swinging to redeliver it
If killing you is the welcome mat I need to get free then I'm finding it
Because I'm walking up out of here today by any means necessary
One... Two... Three... Four... Five... Six...
Seven... Eight... Nine... Ten...
BREATHE
Again.......

Breaking Through Secrets Never Told

Stair after stair I saw you falling
Wall after wall I heard you hit
Bruise after bruise I saw you heal
While surrounded by broken glass you sit

Bone after bone I saw being broken
Crutch after crutch I watched you use
Excuse after excuse was all I heard
Forced to hide the abuse

Hit by your car I watched you fall
Now crying and crawling away
As it comes running through the hall
To hurt you more that day

I sat outside trying to be strong
For I knew what was to come
I went away soon to return
Now my body's growing numb

So year after year I watched it happen
Each time it grew worse
But it was a secret I had to bare
While it raved, and fought, and cursed

Now it's moved on
And into a door your daughter goes
Not knowing who's next I run and hide
Still saying all of this and nobody knows

With a threat on your life you flee
Soon again to appear
Then you lock the doors and attempt to hide
But it breaks in and finds you lurking near

Now through the hall and down the stairs
I watch your body being thrown
As I hear you scream in pain
Now silently walking through where you've flown

Meanwhile your scared children
Cry run mama run away
Not wanting to leave your babies
You reply "for the children I must stay"

Then to alcohol you turned
For a solution not found
And the children bare the pain
Without ever making a sound

Now to your weak and sickened body
So secretly I now tend
Hoping somewhere along the line
Your broken heart I can mend

But God said it's time to go
"I can't leave my babies" you yell
They're strong they'll be okay
But they're going through so much hell

So in a casket I place your body
Never letting out a cry
Still not understanding
I just keep asking why

Free from pain I watched you go
With your savior hand-in-hand

He couldn't take the pain you suffered
So now I understand

I want to go, take me too
I'd often beg and plead
But here I had to stay
So I'd try to take my life figuring it's something I don't need

Then full of anger and rage
Down the road of destruction I turned
Giving up everything to the world
And for years that's where I learned

Then God came back and said "that's enough"
My child hurt no more
With holy hands you saved me
And to sin you closed the door

Turning my life into a testimony
Of all I've overcome
Not focusing on the dark clouds over me
That keep purring out the secrets I desperately tried to run from

After time I lost my sight
As the hurt it all unfolds
And my tears now freely fall
As the secrets are slowly told

Out of my mind I feel I'm going
Deprived of sleep I continuously lay
Wondering sometimes hoping
This is my last day

But through all the feelings
I pray after all you know what's best
And somehow I've convinced myself
It's just another test

So by force I keep going on
Through all my misery and pains of life
Praying for peace and strength
Day by day I live my life.

He Cried

He cried for beating me
And I believed the sincerity in his tears
He bought me gifts and said he loved me
But his raging fists still flew enforcing my fear

He told me he was sorry
He didn't mean it, it wouldn't happen again
But as soon as he was pissed
My head he'd try to cave in

In a heated rage my love for him he couldn't see
Bruises, broken bones, and barely moving
I couldn't think about me
He was sorry….. He loved me

He'd beg me to stay and so I did
I thought my love could change him
So I hid the scars and bruises
And pretended to be ok

The lies we tell and the secrets we keep
Can often times be the difference between living and breathing
And the next hit being the last breath we breathe
Love him enough to walk away
Instead of letting the cycle repeat

You Don't Say

You say you don't want to hurt me
But every time you look at me there's residue of tears on my face
Pain in my heart
And too much confusion to take
You say you love me
Yet I'm always in last place
And your feelings are hard to trace
I'm a faded image in your brain
But I'm the only person to blame
After all I allow this pain
I deal myself a hand in every game
And you'd think I'd be tired of fading into nothing
Not even a memory stain
While you leave your marks that are labeled as claim
And I say to myself you have to go through something to get somewhere
Or every relationship has its test…
But now I'm starting to see this shit is nothing but a mess
Addicted to you physically since I can't unlock you mentally
And emotionally you only give me half the key
So I'm not sure what kind of love I'm caught up in
But it can't be the type of love I used to believe in
Cause I'm hurting while you're still flirting
I'm looking dumb because you're just having fun
And I'm crying while you're half trying
You say you don't want to let me go
You claim it's because you know I'm a good woman
But is it because you think you're lucky and you don't deserve me?
Or are you afraid that someone else can treat me how I should be?
You say you know when something's wrong
But you never realize that it's something you've done
I wish you could see
But I do now.

And I'm not quite sure how I was blinded by the little things
And didn't see the biggest of them all...
I'm selling myself short
Allowing this hurt by a man who still wants to be a boy
And it seems at times you're only in love with the thought of me
The thought that I'd give my last even if you didn't ask
Or how I'd lay down my life just to hear you laugh
Cooking, cleaning, and putting out, playing house
And I'm not even your wife
Keys to my house
Permission to come and go as you please
Raw dogging, and sometimes getting to my knees
Complete control of my emotions and physical being
And then there was her, but that's a different poem
Now don't get me wrong or misread this
When you said "I love you" I believed it, still do
When you said you needed me I knew
And when you placed my hands inside of yours whispering prayers
every night I was blessed to have you...
But you admitted it yourself
You're just not ready for this life
You say I've helped you grow and learn so much
I'm glad I could be of assistance
But I'm done selling myself short at the benefit of someone else...
And I hate to be selfish
But I'm not staying in this game to get hurt
I deserve more
And though I love you tonight
One day somebody's going to love me with all their might.

If You Wasn't My Cousin

His hands kept scrolling over my body
Telling me to relax
That he'd never hurt me
Yea since we shared the same blood
Same tree line
Same grandma and grandpa
But yet here we were
Or here I was...
Stranded in this position trying to think of a way out
His hands massaged areas that were pure
While I tried to back away even more into my pinned corner
He kept talking...
Girl if you wasn't my cousin
If I wasn't... What?
You'd hit me upside the head
Bruise my skin a little
To get what you wanted
What?!
The grimy fingers connected to his hands unpeeled my clothes
The whole time my mouth opened trying to scream
Anyone help please
My body fell limp as his unfortunately stood alert
Girl if you wasn't my cousin...
But yet I am and here we are anyway
You plunging your body on me
Forcing your fingers in and around me
Picking me like bones in fish
We are cousins!!!
I couldn't even yell
As he kept peeling my protection away
Holding my hands with force
Eyes burning red not even noticing my tears bleed.
We are cousins!!!

Sadly this isn't the first time in my family or any other family...
If you wasn't my little sister's daughter...
If you wasn't my wife's child…
If you wasn't my brother's son...
If you wasn't my cousin...

Tug-a-War

Pulling petals off flowers to decide an answer to a question I already knew
I love myself... I hate myself... I love myself... I hate myself...
And the reassurance was painful as I got to the last flower
I love myself
I hate myself
An answer I already knew
I mean look at my arm I keep tally marks of the hate I grew accustomed too
Slow long cuts to help relieve the pain I was going through
I... she... who I am everyday
Never learned how to love the hurt away
But I learned to cope
Crashing and smashing into mirrors
Hateful to you... my reflection

I repeat what I was taught to say to me
You're ugly, You're damaged
Nobody loves you not even me
You're stupid
Look at you you're not even cute
I'm not sure who beauty was but I often wonder why she missed me
I look in the shattered pieces of glass at the
distorted image that stares back at me
And search for the beauty
As I'm frantically searching she notices my scars
and for the first time someone tells me
I'm Beautiful
She pulls the broken pieces from my hand and tells me again
I'm Beautiful
Then lists the reasons one by one on how she came to her conclusion
I quickly interrupted what I thought was an illusion
But she stopped me

And said tell me five things about you that are beautiful
And I couldn't name any

So every day she proceeded to tell me about my beauty
Until I could see it for myself
I was never ugly my beauty was just hidden
behind long cuts and rigged scars
Behind the lies that didn't want me to see it
But now I can list my five things that make me beautiful
My smile because it can help someone else smile
My eyes because they tell a story that needs to be told
My laugh because it's the sound of music in my soul
My skin because that alone contains all the beauty within
My arms because they reveal the secrets
that I was too afraid to whisper
And every day I tell myself
I love myself
I love myself
I love myself
So that I'll always remember

Normal

It's so easy to say that we didn't do it
While we didn't do anything to stop it either
I used to wonder if never speaking up made me just as guilty
So today I speak up and overturn my own convictions

I never tried to explain because it wasn't normal
And you'd never know how I feel
Or that of any normal injured human being
Betrayed by someone we sort of kind of knew
Not a stranger, but the person with the strange
thought who wished to do the abnormal
Plagued with an ongoing fear, a damage deep within
That we don't ever realize we're standing in it….
He used to wonder why I stared blankly at him
Sometimes looking deep within real human eyes was a scare
Dreaming of the future while nightmaring about the
daughter I don't have yet being normal like her mother
Leading to bruises and insecurities you never forget
That's not normal, but normal is abnormal
And then again who ever said molestation was a normal thing
Or that rape should be society's friend?

And they label it as a disease.
Some type of sickness that lead them to do this
Realize being sick is normal; it's a cough or a sneeze
Not a head case forcing his way through and in
I wish they wouldn't make pain, damage,
and destruction a normal thing!
And we want so bad to believe that the monster
is creeping under the bed or in the closet
When they're really the one laying in the
bedroom down the hall from you

The one bold enough to smile in your face and
pretend that everything is normal
And I don't know when normal became touching
privates of young boys and girls
Or when it became him shoving her against
the wall taking whatever he pleased
While normal was too afraid to tell a soul….
Since that night my normal self too tired and too weak to fight back
Because pain never contained strength within my gifts walls
And like many girls before me and
unfortunately more to come after me
It was normal to take part of the blame
Believing we only led it on, encouraged it in some type of way
Too brainwashed that nothing was said
Fear of convicting ones self when a closed
mouth was the worst jail cell
He hurt me, crushed a deep part inside of me
And while my wings flutter now, there was a
time I thought I could never fly again
Flying isn't normal for a regular black girl like me
But then again who ever said molestation was a normal thing
Or that rape should be society's friend…

And I used to feel lost and alone until I read that over
207, 000 people are sexually assaulted every year
Wonder if that includes normal people like me
Too afraid to say anything or too confused,
too hurt, too broken, too unsure
Too full of pain and denial; swear it really didn't happen
Nightmares
Except no matter how many times and different ways I say the lie
My inner thigh always finds a way to cry…
I used to be broken, damaged goods, a butterfly with only one wing
Because it wasn't normal for black girls like me to fly
So I whispered my secret to only one, and he erased the lie
And helped me find the other wing to fly, no to soar
Smile never cry, its normal that butterflies fly

The Stories Lie Within The Pages

Can I make my precious pages cry since I cannot?
Will they express what I can't if I write on
them what's going through my bones?
The fluid that has replaced my red blood
Or the blankness that is now seen in my eyes
What about the crookedness of my smile that
will never shine again, not for you to see
Will my pages read the story of my life, that I refuse to speak?
The things I've seen but never said to anyone
Gun violence, rape, drug abuse, the concrete being my bed
A body waiting for death's arms reaching out
I wonder were they reaching for me or was it
for God to take him into His arms
I pray at night that it was so God could hold
him close, like I do my pillow
But still it makes my soul ache thinking on that night
I cried myself to sleep for weeks to come
Woke up unsure of why God blessed me to see the sun
Pages I ask you, explain it to me so I can understand
Write the stories in my blood, in my tears, and the pees from my fears
I peed in the bed after I saw her with that needle
I was so scared I didn't know what to do
Stood there frozen to the ground eyes didn't
even blink once, much less twice
The look in her eyes was a surprise;
Happiness mixed with the sorrow of the sun
going down never to rise again
I held her close to me and tried to shake her high,
But it was too late because there she closed her yes
And in my arms she laid to rest and woke up
the next morning smile on her face
I was terrified thought she had died
Part of her had thanks to me she said and we walked to the park

Swung high on the swings, thought I'd touch the sky
Laughed like there was no tomorrow and smiled
so the world could see my teeth
Loved that day even though I hated it more
My heart had stopped with the spinning of the world
And the wind lay motionless with not a sound near to hear
My eyes locked into pain and strain
Tingling went down my spine to my arms where
it stopped at my fingers twitching unsure;
Nervous of existence and ready for demise
Will my paper tell the stories that lie in my mind,
that I could never let my mouth speak?
Do the pages express the emotion I wouldn't
let slip out of the corners of my eyes
Or the slobber from my mouth when I sleep at peace
When you read this will you understand the complexity of my life?
The ups and downs and turn arounds that made
me want to stretch out, lie down, and die
What about the joys that I cried from laughter?
The smiles that made my cheeks sore and the
look in my eyes when daddy was alive
Pages of my life and my heart, I pray you can
fulfill telling my unheard stories,
And one day I hope to know the stories that
lay behind the eyes not of mine.

Stained

She'd heard the piercing sound
Of metals life taking
And it would stain her heart forever,
With the terrified look on her brother's face
But confusion and unawareness on hers.
Innocent, she sat in the pew and witnessed
The one tear glide from his eye
And questioned the plastered brave smile.
Every car ride meant a stain on the seat.
Her stomach turned and was at discomfort
As the T.V. flashed off with the quickness
Rushed and thrown out the room, she'd seen it;
A demolished vehicle and everything with it.
The man who shed that one tear
Now lead to her sobbing thousands;
A stain to her soul this time.
She'd glanced in the mirror every morning
Looking past her reflection,
Into the live eyes and smile of souls
Not buried with the physical.
Her hands stained in blood
From neglect and beating the mirror

Stains

There Was A Way Out

There was a way out
You see I kept overlooking that these four walls contained a door
And there was a door knob
So for the first time
With a blackened eye and a bruised spirit
I reached for it
And it actually opened
Yes, there was a way out
There was an escape
Some type of passage way
I was tired of the cycle and the statements
If I could just get out of this situation
I was waddling in it
I use to sit in my own four walls
Hiding in my closet
Trying to cover and mask so many lies to go with the fear
You had disguised your love as pain
But there was a way out
And it's been mistaken and unseen by a lot of people
People who are too busy being caught up in this OMG type life
This "I can't believe" kind of life
Or this I have to play the victim constantly life
But MY four walls contained a door
I found a shelter because I couldn't take it anymore
I couldn't take the pain of my kids watching me like this
I couldn't take letting my kids see you as a man beating on me
I couldn't handle watching him hit on my children
So I decided that I was going to take that way out
That I would run through that open door
Grab as much of my belongs as I can

No, just leave it
Grab the kids and just get out
This is not for me
And this will not be it
Those four walls contained a door
They contained a way out just likes yours

You Gon Get This Work

You gon get this work
Keep thinking you can do as you please
Knock me down to my knees
Pull me up only to do it again
Yes sir I am a queen
But don't underestimate I can get mean
Already forgot I wore a crown
My father was a king
He warned me about men who do simple things
Let you kick me and throw me around
But don't worry baby that gold head piece was found
And as soon as I get up off this ground
You gon get this work!

Beaten Woman's Syndrome

She suffered from (BWS) A Beaten Woman's Syndrome
A die slow disease that cripples your mental and your physical
And I traveled with you every step of the way
As I watched you deteriorate
I've ran with your silhouette at night
And lied inside your cold eyes and cried
At the lost gift no longer presentable
I watched your life dwindle away from me with the sun rise
And your grave fall with the sunset
While I was imprinted with the memory you left
of the unworthiness you felt inside
I embraced the hurt of your heart with my soul
in hopes of somehow easing your pain
I took the blows meant for you in hopes you would remain
But you left
Broken hearted you shamefully clouded your mind with disgrace
Closed your eyes and ignored the bruises that
brutally covered the beauty of your face
Bandaged the broken bones of your weakened
body to bring them a slight peace
And covered the hidden secret of the syndrome that never ceased
And I couldn't protect you
I chased your rolling body down spiraling stair
wells and across blood spattered walls
Fell with you through glass windows while wiping filthy red waterfalls
Watched the black shadows of depression and despair
fill you when he yet again took you there
And when love and fear wouldn't let you leave I stayed with you
And brought color to your soulful blues while
feeding misery with a company
that suicide couldn't even keep
And I held on to you
Until our hearts entangled and our breaths became one

And your soul exhaled through my body on a
journey towards a freedom that has yet begun
As your casket lowered with the depletion of our faith
While the syndrome found its next prey
And penetrated the victim that your secret silence didn't save
And I stood by you……..

The Mirror Was Always Hidden

The mirror was always hidden
Like the definition of beauty is always hidden in society
Because we've been so confused defining it as a physical feature
The curve of my back, the hair that I wear, the
way I smile or the look in my eyes
When the reality is, beauty is defined differently by perception
So the mirrors were always hidden
Like the beauty I carried was hidden
Still waiting to be seen by myself before anyone else could imagine
My beauty is outside but it has to come from the inside
So mirrors were covered by sheets and whatever else could be found
And the concept of who I was not sound
It was still being played in lullaby's that were never sung
Beauty was still being searched for under
the wrong words in the dictionary
Insecure, Broken, Damaged
Mirrors contain images
But even better they are glass
Instead of the reflection being its purpose
It can serve as a way for me cut the broken pieces away
To carve my body into what I need it to be
What I want to see when I glue broken pieces back together and
stare at incomplete images of me

Porcelain Doll

Broken hearts don't always mend
And it's sad
That we can only wait for the bleeding to stop
For a pain that hardly ever ends
Shattered pieces of life we dreamed
And band aids that decorate the heart
Like burettes in little black girl's hair
What about the scars?
That are forever penetrated in my eyes
Footprints that you left across my face
As I search for the glass pieces
Thrown to the floor
Didn't you know the heart's like a porcelain doll?
Priceless and break too easy

Take a Deeper Look

Come take a deeper look into my eyes and see the life I've lead
Back when I was willing to do anything just to stay ahead
Come join me on my journey down a path that I once knew
To a secret life I lived and everything I went through
Come see the world where I fought my way through life
To the heart that bottled all the saddest devastations of my life
See the beatings I witnessed, the ones that made violence all I knew
Where I act as those I saw, so if you hit me I hit you too
Look a little deeper at the violent child I was
That became a crazy teenager who tortured herself just because
Look at that same girl who's now strung out on drugs
After finding her parents dead moments after giving them a hug
Now look at her with the liquor bottles in her hand
Trying to act as if nothing bothers her
looking for completeness in a man
Look at all the hurt that is written on her face
As she tries to take her life thinking there must be a better place
Yes, come look a little deeper at her body now bearing a child
Now bleeding in a hospital bed miscarrying
thinking it was cause she was so wild
Now she's got a friend who beats her black and blue
As she turns to the Lord to help her make it through
As you study look deep I want you to see through my eyes
At the young woman who is now nobody's prize
As you've taken a deeper look into the secret life I had
I hope you think twice about things when you're so called mad
Stop being so quick to judge me based off the things you see
And learn to take a deeper look cause the
cover doesn't tell the whole story

Nigga Get Gone

Nigga where you at?
Where the hell you been?
I been calling
Even called your friends
You wouldn't answer your phone
Your cell, or my page
Yet you expect me to be locked in this house
Like a dog confined to its cage

While you want to kick it
Stay out late, and play these games
Then come creepin' in me
Like shit still the same
Now it's time to quit you
One last hit then leave
I'm not with these stories
Your lies I can't receive

You said you wasn't side stepping
But its 6 a.m and ya ass still gone
Work ended at 5 and the clubs closed at 2
Nigga…. GET YA SHIT and get gone
Where you gonna stay?
That ain't my concern
I warned you once
Now you gonna learn

Go live with Shantell, Janet, Sharee
Whoever you been layed up with
I don't give a damn where you go
But you better call Tyrone cause you getting the hell up out my shit

So you think you bad, you wanna hit me
Stuntin' for ya friends
Now they're dressed up crying
Cause your funeral's where they been
I told the nigga to get gone
Nigga wanna play these games
In my house I call the shots
And in court self-defense was my only claim

I Didn't Need Marks To Remind Me How Much I Hated Myself

I didn't need marks to remind me how much I hated myself
Pain was already a normal thing for me
It was my shirt my jeans my shoes and a piece of cloth I wore that day
Even better it was the scars that marked my arms
Since every time I hugged you it was like glass scratching at me
It would never last this love we have
This love lust pretend truth lie love that we had
It was insecure so I'd hold you cutting myself more
But you seemed stable
secure except you were a wobbly table barely standing on all five of your own legs
I still clung to you and allowed you to cut the insides of me
The inside of my arms the inside of my thighs
We had drank too much and somehow you thought you could take what wasn't yours
You had climbed and crawled into place that was sacred
It didn't belong to you
I feel partially to blame because I gave up the fight
I gave in to you because I was too tired
We would never be the same
Things would never be the same
My dorm room would always feel violated
And then there are the scars inside my thigh
Those are hard to cover up not like the ones on my arms
The scars that you left on me
Cloths of pain weren't enough to cover them up
And hurt didn't drape the way it needed to drape
I was left standing naked looking at my mirrors reflections
Everyone wondered why I hated myself so much
Not only did I look like that woman

The one that I talk about too much even though I really don't know her
But now I had to deal with looking into more hurt
Because I was stupid enough to play a silly game with a boy
A boy who thought he had more to gain
A boy who swore he could take whatever he wanted
He said he wrote is name on me
His scars became claim
And I thought I'd always be broken hearted
Since scars don't heal as fast as I thought they could
They didn't seem to heal very well
I can still feel them very well
He crawled inside of me
He sat in there like I was him
But he wasn't me
I've been physically abused
And I never said anything
Like most woman I swore it was my fault
That I somehow led him on and made him think it was ok
Maybe if I hadn't leaned the way I did
Or laughed and touched his arm
Or let him touch my lower back when he opened the door
He wouldn't have thought it was ok to leave scars inside my thighs
To allow his jagged glass to cut the inside of my arms
He would've understood that I was worth more than a "my bad, did that hurt"
Or the occasional sorry
What do you mean Yes that hurt
It hurt walking across campus and having uncomfortable moments of seeing him
Bothered that he was flirting with other girls
You didn't even call me after you decided to take a part of me
I was only left with a sorry

I'm so sorry to myself
That I allowed it and justified your treatment
I'm so sorry to myself
That I tried to use cocoa butter to cover up these scars

I look at them now and embrace what they're worth
I realized you were only a testimony
And I will never allow anyone to crawl inside of me
I will never allow anyone to jaggedly cut the inside of me

Tornado

Everything's destroyed
Fires have burned down what was left after the tornado ran through
And I know my tears flooded downstairs
Your fist broke down the wall
I put dents in the oven & the dishwasher with my foot
Everything's destroyed
But for whatever reason we're still sitting here
Looking blankly at one another
Trying to figure out who started this war
And who let the tornado in the door?
Because we both know I lit the fire
Might as well burn the bad memories down
What happened?
We never lived like this
But somehow my love changed you
And if I had known my love would drive you mad
I would have loved you the same
Maybe harder, but not softer…
But who started this war?
Who decided that our love was out of control
That it was too much and that they needed to shed blood
Who fired the first shot,
And who let the tornado in the door?
Because we both know I lit the fire
Only because you punched down the walls
And split my heart in two
Only because you didn't know how to control love
And keep mistaking it for abuse
It was like my kisses were like kicks
That my hugs felt like I was stabbing you
Except you were the one stabbing at me
All I wanted was to love you
And I did, but somehow it turned you into this

Not the same man I met and fell in love with
Some little boy trying to amuse himself by dressing up in his daddy's clothes
Us playing pretend to be in love not even sure if we liked each other at the moment
And our bedroom walls holding love, pain, torture, and too much nonsense
We never spoke about the changes, only shrugged and kept going
Swept it under the rug until I flooded down stairs with my tears
And who let the tornado in the door?
Because we both know I lit the fire
We sit in a destroyed house
Only staring at each others' blankness…
So I guess I'll be the first to move
And I'll walk out because there ain't no point in staying
Trying to piece back broken memories that were already shredded
Since we only wanted to remember bits and pieces
Of course only the good things…
But before I leave, let me take a look around
Get a good picture of the hearts on the ceiling,
The poetry that was written in our sheets,
The love that was baked in our oven that now has my foot's indention,
And the look in your eyes
I would say a funny joke to remember your smile
But instead I'll make walking away easier
Because there ain't no starting over…
I open what's left of our front door to say,
"I know she let the tornado in the door?
Because we both know I lit the fire."

Pain, Suffering, and Sorrow

She talks about pain, suffering, and sorrow
Yet is still hopeful things will get better tomorrow
Every day her heart is heavy and she's trembling with fear
She's continuously jumping from every noise she hears
Her mind is cluttered with the things we can't see
Her mother couldn't take it and decided to OD
Because she walked in on her husband playing doctor in places
he should never be
And later discovered her brother plays there too
There's just some things in life a little girl
should never have to go through
But every day she's forced to keep a fake smile on her face
Still hoping that tomorrow everything will be ok
Silently crying out while trying to be strong
Hoping her rescuer would soon be coming along
But with no one to protect her she just kept going through
Then her silence killed her before she could talk to you
They completely broke her spirit and she could take no more
This time when they came for her she was dead on the bathroom floor

Troubles Don't Last Always

I know your mind is troubled
And your eyes cry tears of pain
I know your heart is aching
And all you see are clouds of rain

But your days will soon get better
And your pain will go away
And God will still be at your side
Once your troubles have gone astray.

Let Me Be Me

Let me think
Let me breathe
Just let me be me
When my world fell apart
That's when my heart started
Started to love or to hate
No one knows, not even me
But my mind wondered a 1000 times
And my soul sought every second of life
The eyes I looked out of were no longer fogged
And the clearness of the day I could see
I thought life had had me down
But I was nowhere near the ground
Could I have been under it?
I may never know,
But I do know now
Just where I stand
On my shadow
In a place all its own
In never ever land…
Let me live
Let me fly
Just let me be me
Floating off in the clouds
Mind in the deepest gutter
And lips won't even utter
To a soul
Broken and unbroken
Torn but taped together
In a world all its own

I look in the mirror to see my reflection,
Realize... I am my reflection
Or is she me?
No one knows, not even I
And my heart beats 2000 times
As my mind searches every step taken,
Ears open waiting for the whispers of the world
The sound of laughter in the cool breeze
Let me smile
Let me hide
Just let me be me!

Brain Surgeon

I know you see these scars
Small cracks and cuts mentally
So you can imagine why I'm hesitant to let you "fix" things
I have seen what knives can do when placed in the wrong hands
Hands of family
Friends
Myself
And strangers I thought I knew
People who were supposed to protect me
The person who I thought was created to love me

I understand you call yourself a doctor
And you feel as though you have healing powers
But you have to understand these scars before brain surgery can be done
Map out the plan for what needs to be done

My occipital lobe has seen so much my pain
I wear glasses because my brain's been shook and no longer wants to see clearly
Because even my dreams have turned into nightmares
Like those little girls have when someone did something they shouldn't have done
Since two letter words no longer carry a meaning
And NO seemed to turn into ON
I think they were dyslexic confusing letters voice tone and swinging fists
Doctor my occipital lobe is primarily the problem because I have seen so much
Dreamed myself out of touch
It's cancer spread to the temporal lobe and scarred my long term memory
I'll never forget my childhood
The moments you forgot to hug me and tell me you loved me
Bedtime stories that were read to other children
And the unawareness of the damage that should be considered a sin

There are missing pieces of my memory like my mother's scent and maybe her smile
Laughter from my father and lessons neither taught
My temporal lobe memory is missing my parents
And my stand in parents didn't see me as their child
Our blood line wasn't thicker than water that grew money
All of this has damaged my frontal lobe
My personality is a reflection of a lot of the damage that's been done
I have emotionally cut myself
Destroyed and carved an image until there was nothing left
Boxed feelings into a four walled room and overlooked that there was a door
That's when fear controlled my whole mind and body
Doctor the problem is also in my cerebellum
I was afraid that I could be my own light in the darkness
And that fear still plagues me today
I don't know how to trust because those who I did couldn't commit
Selfless for selfish people
Confusion plays tricks on this part of my brain
What I thought was pleasure turned into pain
The same people hurting me over and over again
I told you earlier that knives can be dangerous
But even more ripping out my heart and placing it into the hands of strangers
Keep it safe please don't drop my porcelain piece
Listen closely when I say I have some scars that need to be healed
More on the inside than the outer layers
But I need brain surgery because my whole brain experiences what only the parietal lobe should feel
PAIN
So doctor
I came to you today with hopes that you'll treat my brain better than my heart has been
I've been abused in too many ways
So if we can start healing the mental pain I think there's more to gain
I'm terrified with you and those scissors
But I trust you when you say you've come to heal

Resources

Below you will find a list of resources that have been helpful to either or both authors of Fists of Rage. If you or someone you know is in need of assistance to get free of a current or past experience, please utilize these resources. The situations written about in the poems that you have read are serious and real. Please do not ignore any need for help going forward. You now have no excuse.

<u>National Assistance</u>

Rainn.org

Thehotline.org

Loveisrepect.org

<u>Local Assistance in DFW</u>

Genesis Women's Shelter (214) 946-HELP 24 hour hotline

New Beginning Center (972) 276-0057 hotline www.newbeginningcenter.org

At the Table Counseling (214) 684-5867 www.atthetablecounseling.com

www.ingramcontent.com/pod-product-compliance
Lightning Source LLC
Chambersburg PA
CBHW060342080526
44584CB00013B/887